The Successful Path of Consultants:

Unleash Your Wealth and Leave Legacy

James D. Hudson

Table Of Content

Introduction

The world of consulting has undergone a transformative shift, with the traditional image of a consultant evolving into that of a wealthy consultant, a professional known not only for their financial success but also for their unparalleled expertise, strategic acumen, and ability to navigate complex business environments.

This introduction dives into the attributes that distinguish a wealthy consultant, as well as the changing nature of the job.

A rich consultant is essentially someone who has perfected the art of delivering strategic advice while also achieving financial success. Unlike traditional consultants, who may only focus on problem solving, the affluent consultant takes a holistic approach to their job, incorporating a wide range of abilities that extend beyond the standard boundaries of consulting.

The wealthiest consultant's success is built on their expertise. These individuals are often experts in specialized industries or niches, with a thorough awareness of the complexities and challenges unique to such domains.

Whether it's financial consulting, technological advisory, or management consulting, the affluent consultant's knowledge base is both broad and deep, allowing them to deliver vital insights and solutions to their clients.

Strategic thinking is another distinguishing feature of a prosperous consultant. Beyond tackling urgent difficulties, these people excel at seeing the larger picture and developing unique solutions for their clients.

Wealthy consultants stand out from their peers because they can analyze complex circumstances, discover opportunities, and build complete plans.

They do more than just supply solutions; they create routes for long-term growth and achievement.
Adaptability is an important skill in the consulting industry, and affluent consultants exemplify this quality.

The corporate environment is always evolving, impacted by technical advances, market volatility, and global events. A rich consultant is skilled in navigating this dynamic market, staying ahead of trends, and adapting their approach to changing client needs.

This adaptability extends not only to technical capabilities but also to good communication, interpersonal interactions, and the flexibility to work smoothly across varied industries.

Client pleasure is the ultimate metric for a wealthy consultant's success. Aside from financial rewards, these professionals develop their reputation by having a tangible impact on their clients' company.

Whether streamlining processes, executing radical changes, or resolving complicated challenges, the affluent consultant's work demonstrates their capacity to provide real and verifiable value. Client satisfaction also serves as the foundation for long-term partnerships, which frequently result in repeat business and recommendations, demonstrating the consultant's lasting impact.

Ethical considerations are important to the identity of a wealthy consultant. As trusted consultants, these experts manage sensitive information and traverse complex organizational systems.

Maintaining the greatest ethical standards, such as secrecy, integrity, and transparency, is critical. A wealthy consultant's success is assessed not just in money gains, but also in the ethical ideals that guide their professional behavior.

Finally, the introduction to the affluent consultant reveals a dynamic and complex profession that extends beyond traditional concepts of consulting.

These experts represent a distinct combination of competence, strategic thinking, adaptability, client satisfaction, and ethical behavior.

As businesses face new difficulties and seek counsel in an ever-changing landscape, the position of the rich consultant is poised to become increasingly important, defining the future of consulting and contributing to the success of organizations around the world.

Chapter 1

Getting On the Right Track for Consulting Success

In the fast-paced world of consulting, success demands a strategic strategy that combines skill, networking, and ongoing self-improvement.

This book attempts to provide insights into the important components that lead to a successful consulting career and a road to profitability in the business.

1. Developing Expertise

To succeed in consulting, one must gain deep experience in a given topic.

Continuous learning, maintaining current with industry developments, and gaining necessary credentials are essential.
A well-rounded skill set boosts your credibility and marketability.

2. Effective Networking:

Networking is critical to consultancy success. Building and cultivating relationships with clients, coworkers, and industry leaders can lead to opportunities.

Attend conferences, join professional associations, and use social media to broaden your network.

3. Customer Relationship Management:

The capacity to cultivate excellent client relationships is critical to success in consulting. Understand their needs, consistently provide value, and communicate openly. Client satisfaction typically leads to repeat business and referrals, which contribute to long-term success.

4. Strategic Marketing

Position yourself as an authority through thought leadership, blogs, and public speaking opportunities.

A good personal brand increases your exposure and attracts customers. Create a captivating web presence to highlight your abilities and set yourself apart in a competitive market.

5. Adaptability And Innovation

The consulting landscape is changing rapidly. Embrace change, remain adaptable, and be open to innovation.

This approach keeps your solutions relevant, distinguishing you as a consultant who understands the nuances of the business world.

6. Financial Management

Prosperity necessitates proper financial management. Create explicit pricing structures, meticulously manage project budgets, and ensure timely billing.

A strong financial strategy supports your consulting practice's long-term profitability and growth.

7. Collaboration Among The Team.

Building a successful consulting practice frequently necessitates collaboration with others. Create a collaborative and inclusive workplace atmosphere.

Recognize team members' strengths, allocate responsibilities effectively, and develop an environment that fosters creativity and success.

8. Continuous Improvement

Successful consultants are committed to continuous learning and progress. Get feedback from clients and peers, assess your performance, and identify areas for improvement.

This commitment to self-improvement keeps you ahead in a competitive consulting landscape.

Conclusion

Consulting success involves a combination of experience, networking, client management, marketing, adaptability, financial acumen, team collaboration, and a dedication to continuous development. By embracing these crucial components, consultants can establish a healthy practice and achieve long-term success in the dynamic consulting industry.

Building a Solid Foundation for Consultant Success

In the fast-paced and competitive world of consulting, success is more than just providing outstanding services; it is also about laying a solid foundation that will support and propel your career.

Aspiring and experienced consultants can both benefit from a deliberate approach to developing a solid foundation for success.

Let's look at the important components that lead to a strong foundation for consultant success.

1. Identify Your Purpose And Values.

A successful consulting career begins with a clear sense of purpose and values.

Define the influence you wish to have and the concepts that will govern your efforts. This foundation serves as a compass, guiding you toward actions that are in line with your personal and professional goals.

2. Determine Your Niche.

Specialization is essential for consultant success. Find a niche in which your expertise may genuinely shine. Whether it's strategy, technology, or a certain business, carving out a niche allows you to stand out, establish a name, and attract clients looking for specialised knowledge.

3. Invest In Education And Skills Development.

Continuous learning is essential for every effective consultant. Stay current with industry trends, learn new skills, and pursue relevant certifications.

A dedication to study not only expands your knowledge but also positions you as a consultant who provides cutting-edge solutions to clients.

4. Establish A Strong Professional Network.
Networking is a critical component of consultant success. Develop relationships with coworkers, clients, and industry leaders.

Attend conferences, join professional groups, and participate in online communities.

A strong network provides not just commercial chances, but also assistance and information.

5. Improve Communication Skills.
Communication is key to the consulting process. Improve your capacity to clearly communicate complicated ideas, actively listen to customer demands, and adjust your communication style to different audiences.

Effective communication fosters trust and ensures that your recommendations are received and implemented.

6. Adopt A Client-Centered Approach.

Understanding and meeting the needs of the client is critical to consulting success. Take a client-centric approach by actively listening, anticipating difficulties, and providing solutions that exceed expectations.

Prioritizing the client experience not only increases satisfaction, but it also leads to long-term connections and repeat sales.

7. Develop a Strong Work Ethic

Consultant success is generally associated with a strong work ethic. Show dependability, fulfill deadlines on a continuous basis, and go above and above to provide value.

A strong work ethic establishes a reputation for reliability and professionalism, which pave the way for long-term success.

8.Implement Efficient Project Management.

Successful consulting requires effective project management. Develop great organizational skills, establish realistic project timeframes, and manage resources efficiently.

A well-executed project not only pleases clients, but it also helps you build a reputation as a results-oriented consultant.

9. Prioritize Personal Well-Being.

Professional achievements are not the only way to assess success. Maintain a good work-life balance to put your well-being first.

Set limits, take pauses, and engage in things that will replenish your mind and body. A balanced existence fosters long-term success in the hard business of consulting.

10. Seek And Learn From Feedback.

Feedback is an important tool for improvement. Actively solicit input from customers, coworkers, and mentors. Use constructive criticism to improve your abilities and strategies.

A dedication to ongoing development based on feedback ensures that you stay versatile and resilient throughout your consulting career.

Building a solid foundation for consultant success requires a combination of personal growth, specialized knowledge, good communication, and a client-focused attitude.

Investing in these core pieces not only positions you for immediate success, but also creates a durable and long-lasting platform for future successes in the dynamic world of consulting.

Strategic Steps to Prosperity in Consulting

Successful consulting demands a planned and strategic approach. Whether you're an individual consultant or part of a consulting business, taking important strategic actions can pave the path for long-term success.

Let's take a look at the steps that make up a complete consulting success strategy.

1. Identify Your Niche and Expertise.

A well-defined specialization serves as the cornerstone for a successful consulting career.

Determine your area of specialization, the industry in which you shine, and the unique challenges you can address.

A specific emphasis not only distinguishes you, but also helps you to expand your expertise and become a sought-after expert.

2. Develop a Unique Value Proposition.

Clearly describe what distinguishes you from other consultants. Create a convincing value proposition that showcases your unique abilities, expertise, and the specific value you provide to clients.

This will be the foundation of your marketing activities and an important aspect in acquiring customers.

3. Establish A Strong Online Presence.

Having a solid online presence is critical in today's digital world. Create a professional website, improve your LinkedIn profile, and highlight your experience through blogs, articles, or case studies.

A strong internet presence not only draws new customers, but it also increases your industry reputation.

4. Invest in Continuous Learning.

The consulting industry is ever-changing. Invest in constant learning to stay ahead of the curve. Attend industry conventions, take appropriate courses, and remain current on developing trends.

A dedication to continued education keeps your skills relevant and places you as a consultant at the forefront of your area.

5. Build A Strong Network.

Networking is a valuable advantage in consulting. Develop ties with people in your field, attend networking events, and use social media. A strong network may lead to recommendations, collaborations, and useful insights that help you succeed.

6. Use Effective Marketing Strategies.

Create a detailed marketing plan specific to your target demographic. Use both online and offline platforms to contact potential prospects. This might involve content marketing, social media campaigns, and participation at industry events. Consistent and targeted marketing activities will increase your market exposure.

Chapter 2

Building Financial Success in Consulting

In the realm of consulting, achieving financial success requires a combination of strategic planning, financial acumen, and business foresight. Whether you're an independent consultant or part of a consulting firm, establishing a strong financial foundation is essential for long-term prosperity.

Let's explore key strategies for building financial success in the dynamic field of consulting.

1. Set Clear Financial Goals

Building financial success begins with setting clear and measurable goals. Define both short-term and long-term financial objectives for your consulting career.

Whether it's achieving a specific income level, increasing profit margins, or saving for future investments, having well-defined goals provides a roadmap for your financial journey.

2. Establish a Robust Budget

A fundamental step in financial success is creating a detailed budget. Track income, expenses, and allocate resources strategically.

This not only ensures that you live within your means but also allows for intentional saving and investment.

A well-structured budget is a cornerstone for financial stability and growth.

3. Diversify Income Streams

Consulting success is often enhanced by diversifying income streams.

In addition to client projects, explore opportunities for passive income, such as creating and selling digital products, offering online courses, or writing books.

Diversification minimizes financial reliance on a single source and provides stability in varying market conditions.

4. Implement Effective Pricing Strategies

Pricing your consulting services appropriately is crucial for financial success. Consider the value you provide, market demand, and competitive rates when determining your pricing strategy.

Regularly review and adjust your pricing to reflect your expertise and the changing dynamics of the consulting landscape.

5. Build a Solid Emergency Fund

Financial stability in consulting is contingent on having a safety net. Establish and maintain an emergency fund that covers three to six months' worth of living expenses.

This fund provides a financial cushion during lean periods or unexpected challenges, allowing you to weather uncertainties without compromising your financial health.
6. Invest Strategically

Smart investing is a key component of building financial success. Research and consider diverse investment options, such as stocks, bonds, real estate, or retirement accounts. Seek the guidance of financial advisors if needed.

Investments can generate passive income and contribute significantly to your long-term financial goals.

7.   Prioritize Client Relationship Management:

Building and sustaining excellent client connections is essential. Pay close attention to clients' needs, communicate openly, and provide solutions that surpass expectations.

Clients that are satisfied not only return business, but they also become ambassadors for your services, recommending them to others.

8. Expand Your Service Offerings

Diversification is generally associated with prosperity. Consider increasing your service offerings in response to market demand and your developing expertise.

This not only broadens your customer base but also establishes you as a flexible consultant capable of resolving a wide variety of company issues.

9. Implement Scalable Systems

Scalable solutions for managing processes, client interactions, and administrative chores should be implemented as your consulting firm expands.

Efficiency and scalability help to long-term profitability by allowing you to handle rising workloads while focusing on high-value tasks.

10. Evaluate and Adapt

Evaluate your consultancy business's performance on a regular basis. Analyze client comments, check financial indicators, and keep track of market developments.

Use this knowledge to adjust your plans, fine-tune your approach, and keep your consulting practice current with the ever-changing corporate landscape.

Finally, success in consulting stems from strategic strategy and implementation. You may design a plan for long-term success in the consulting profession by defining your expertise, developing a strong web presence, investing in ongoing learning, managing client relationships, and adjusting to market trends. Each strategic phase adds to the overall strategy, bringing you to a successful and rewarding consulting career.

A practical guide on wealth management strategies for consultants.

Consulting is a vibrant and lucrative career, but financial success takes more than just providing excellent service.

Wealth management is a vital component that allows consultants to establish and maintain their financial well-being throughout their careers.

In this practical book, we will look at critical wealth management methods that are targeted to the specific issues and possibilities that consultants encounter.

1. Understand Your Cash Flow

Wealth management starts with a solid grasp of your financial flow. Track your income and spending carefully in order to uncover patterns and opportunities for improvement.

This knowledge enables you to organize resources more efficiently, ensuring that you have enough money to meet your personal and professional obligations.

2. Develop a comprehensive budget.

A well-structured budget is the cornerstone for successful asset management. Categorize your costs, prioritize your financial objectives, and distribute cash accordingly.

Your budget should be reviewed and adjusted on a regular basis to reflect changes in income, spending, or financial goals. A dynamic budget acts as a road map for your financial progress.

3. Create an Emergency Fund.

Consultants frequently encounter varying project flow. Establishing and maintaining an emergency fund is critical.

Set aside three to six months' worth of living costs in a liquid account. This safety net gives financial stability during lean periods or unexpected setbacks, helping you to handle uncertainty with confidence.

4. Invest in Professional Development.

Your experience is a valuable resource. Invest in continuous professional development to improve your abilities and keep on top of industry developments.

This strategic investment not only enhances your consulting skills, but also prepares you for higher-paying possibilities and long-term financial success.

5. Diversify your income streams.

Diversification is essential to financial stability. In addition to client assignments, consider generating digital goods, delivering training sessions, or publishing industry-related material.

Diversifying income decreases reliance on a single source and ensures stability in volatile market situations.

6. Optimize Tax Strategies.

Tax efficiency is an important part of wealth management. Consult with a tax specialist to maximize your tax options.

Take advantage of deductions, look into tax-advantaged retirement plans, and remain up to date on tax law changes. Effective tax planning increases after-tax income and helps to overall financial success.

7. Set Clear Financial Goals.

Setting specific financial objectives is a guiding element in wealth management.

Define short-term and long-term goals, such as obtaining a specific salary level, saving for retirement, or purchasing a home.

Specific, quantifiable goals give guidance and inspiration for your financial pursuits.

8. Conduct regular investment reviews and adjustments.

Review your investment portfolio on a regular basis to verify that it is in line with your financial goals and tolerance for risk.

Rebalance as required, and consider changing your asset allocation based on market circumstances.

Regular monitoring helps you to make educated decisions that help you achieve your long-term wealth-building goals.

9. Implement Risk Management Strategies.

Consultants frequently encounter uncertainty in project availability and economic situations.

Implement risk management tactics to help you avoid future setbacks. This may entail obtaining proper insurance coverage, developing contingency plans, and diversifying your clientele to lessen reliance on certain businesses or sectors.

10. Plan for Retirement Early

Retirement planning is a fundamental aspect of wealth management. Start contributing to retirement accounts early in your employment to get the benefits of compound growth. Look into alternatives such as individual retirement plans (IRAs) and Solo 401(k)s for self-employed consultants. Over time, consistent contributions accumulate into a substantial retirement savings.

11. Seek Professional Financial Advice.

Engage with financial specialists who specialize in collaborating with consultants. A financial adviser may provide tailored guidance, assist with difficult wealth management decisions, and provide insights into investment possibilities that correspond with your objectives. Their experience can help you optimize your financial plans for long-term success.

To summarize, successful wealth management is a proactive and continuing effort for consultants looking for financial success. Consultants may provide a sound financial foundation by assessing cash flow, developing a complete budget, diversifying revenue sources, optimizing tax methods, and planning for retirement. Implementing these practical techniques helps consultants maintain resilience, security, and success throughout their careers.

Diversifying Income Streams and Maximizing Financial Opportunities in Consulting

In the ever-changing consulting market, diversifying revenue streams is a smart technique that may dramatically improve financial stability and open up new development opportunities.

Relying primarily on client projects may restrict prospective earnings and expose consultants to market swings. Consultants may establish a robust and sustainable income strategy by embracing a variety of revenue streams.

1. Consulting Engagements

Client projects continue to be the primary source of income for consultants. Providing specific expertise and services to customers serves as the foundation for a consulting profession. Recognizing the cyclical nature of project-based business, consultants can proactively exploit their abilities and reputation to ensure a consistent flow of engagements.

2. Digital Products and Services.

Consultants can expand their reach by developing and marketing digital goods and services. This might be e-books, online courses, webinars, or downloadable resources pertaining to their niche. Digital goods enable consultants to access a larger audience, create passive revenue, and establish themselves as industry thought leaders.

3. Training and Workshops.

Training sessions and seminars are an effective approach for consultants to share their knowledge and skills.

These training possibilities, whether conducted in-person or virtually, not only provide additional revenue but also increase the consultant's exposure and reputation in the industry.

4. Speaking Engagements.

Consultants can make money by giving public speeches at conferences, industry events, and webinars. Such engagements frequently include speaker fees, sponsorships, and networking possibilities.

Becoming a popular speaker not only diversifies revenue but also positions the consultant as an expert in their industry.

5. Affiliate Marketing

Consultants might explore affiliate marketing by collaborating with businesses that share their expertise.

Recommending suitable items or services to their target audience while receiving commissions on purchases may be a passive but significant source of income. Careful affiliate alliance selection ensures that the consultant's brand and values are aligned.

6. Freelance Writer and Content Creator

Sharing ideas through freelance writing, providing articles to industry periodicals, and developing website content may all be financially profitable.

Consultants may monetize their knowledge by creating high-quality content, garnering a larger audience, and even earning money for their work.

7. Online Platforms and Marketplaces

Consultants can generate additional revenue by leveraging internet platforms and markets.

Offering consulting services or courses on sites such as Upwork, Udemy, or Fiverr may link consultants with a worldwide audience, expanding their earning potential beyond local clients.

8. Collaborations And Partnerships.

Strategic collaborations and partnerships can lead to financial benefits for both sides. This might include co-hosting events, cross-promoting services, or partnering on joint projects.

Such collaborations not only diversify income streams, but they also widen the consultant's network and market access.

9. Subscription Plans and Memberships

Consultants can generate recurring revenue by exploring subscription models or membership programs. Offering unique material, tools, or continuous assistance to a subscription group generates a consistent income while instilling a sense of belonging in customers or followers.

10. Real Estate Investments.

As consultants' financial resources grow, they may consider making real estate investments. Rental properties or real estate crowdfunding can generate passive income and diversify the consultant's investment portfolio, bringing stability to their entire financial plan.

Diversifying income streams is more than just maximizing financial prospects; it is also a risk management approach. Consultants construct a more sustainable income model by diversifying their sources of revenue.

Furthermore, diversification enables consultants to benefit on their skills in a variety of ways, establishing them for long-term success and financial prosperity in the dynamic consulting industry.

Budgeting and fiscal discipline are critical pillars of long-term financial success for consultants.

Budgeting and economic discipline are critical in the complicated dance of consulting, where project timeframes fluctuate and revenue might be intermittent.

These two pillars are the foundation of long-term financial success for consultants, offering stability, foresight, and a road map for accomplishing both personal and professional financial objectives.

1. Creating A Detailed Budget

A well-constructed budget acts as the consultant's financial roadmap. It is more than just managing spending; it is a strategic tool for efficiently allocating resources.

Begin by classifying personal and company expenses, differentiating between fixed and variable costs. Include things such as rent, utilities, insurance, professional memberships, marketing costs, and emergency savings.

A thorough grasp of cash inflows and outflows is essential for making sound financial decisions.

2. Anticipating Uncertain Income

One of the major issues that consultants encounter is inconsistent revenue streams. Budgeting is essential for controlling this unpredictability.

Rather of depending on a steady paycheck, consultants must estimate their typical monthly revenue, plan for lean times, and spend cash accordingly.

Creating a cash reserve for slow months ensures that critical financial commitments are satisfied, which contributes to fiscal stability amid project flow changes.

3. Create Emergency Funds

Fiscal discipline entails planning for unanticipated occurrences. Consultants should prioritize establishing and keeping emergency reserves sufficient to cover at least three to six months of living expenditures.

This safety net serves as a financial buffer during unanticipated downturns, giving consultants peace of mind and helping them to handle obstacles without jeopardizing their financial health.

4. Strategic Debt Management.

While leveraging resources is typical, financial discipline requires advisors to handle debt appropriately. Distinguish between good and bad debt, prioritize high-interest repayments, and avoid incurring excessive liabilities.

A disciplined attitude to debt guarantees that financial resources are channeled toward wealth-building activities rather than debt repayment.

5. Matching Personal and Professional Goals

Budgeting is more than just the bottom line for businesses; it is a comprehensive method that aligns personal and professional financial objectives. Consultants should think about long-term goals like retirement planning, property, or educational investments for themselves or their family. Integrating personal goals into the budgeting process ensures a comprehensive approach to financial discipline.

6. Consistently reviewing and adjusting budgets.

A stagnant budget is a squandered chance for progress. Consultants should take a dynamic approach, assessing and changing their budgets on a frequent basis. Changes in income, spending, or financial goals should drive changes.

This iterative method guarantees that the budget stays relevant and effective, adjusting to the changing nature of the consulting industry.

7. Investing In Professional Development

Fiscal discipline goes beyond the current financial transactions. Investing in professional growth is a smart financial move.

Allocate a percentage of the money to continuing education, certifications, or training that improves consulting abilities. This investment not only prepares the consultant for higher-paying prospects, but it also helps to ensure long-term financial success.

8. Monitoring and Mitigating Risk

Consultants work in a constantly changing environment with inherent dangers. Fiscal discipline entails detecting possible hazards, such as economic downturns, industry shifts, or client reliance.

Consultants' budgets should include risk mitigation methods to provide financial resilience in the face of unanticipated obstacles.

9. Automating Savings And Investments.

Automation of saves and investing can help to strengthen fiscal discipline. Set up automatic transfers to selected savings or investment accounts.

This not only encourages disciplined saving, but it also guarantees that financial goals, such as retirement planning or portfolio development, are constantly met.

10. Seeking Professional Financial Advice.

While consultants excel in their own industries, receiving expert financial advice is a prudent decision. Financial advisers that have worked with consultants can give personalized insights, improve tax methods, and advise on wealth-building prospects.

Their advice adds a layer of experience to budgetary discipline, boosting the consultant's long-term financial success.

Finally, budgeting and fiscal discipline are more than just financial management chores; they are vital cornerstones that ensure consultants' long-term success.

Consultants may negotiate the obstacles of their career with resilience and achieve long-term financial prosperity by adopting strategic budgeting strategies, managing irregular revenue, and establishing disciplined financial habits.

Chapter 3

Strategic Consulting Approaches: Navigating Complexity with Precision

In the ever-evolving landscape of business, strategic consulting has become an indispensable asset for organizations seeking to navigate complexities, overcome challenges, and capitalize on opportunities.

A successful strategic consulting approach goes beyond offering generic solutions; it involves a nuanced understanding of the client's unique context and the application of specialized methodologies.

Here, we delve into key strategic consulting approaches that consultants employ to drive impactful and sustainable change.

1. Comprehensive Research and Analysis

A cornerstone of any effective strategic consulting approach is thorough research and analysis.

Consultants meticulously gather data, assess market trends, and scrutinize internal processes to develop a comprehensive understanding of the client's environment.

This evidence-based foundation serves as the bedrock for informed decision-making and strategic planning.

2. SWOT Analysis

The SWOT analysis, examining an organization's strengths, weaknesses, opportunities, and threats, is a classic but powerful strategic consulting tool. It provides a holistic view of the internal and external factors influencing the business landscape.

Consultants leverage the insights gained from SWOT analysis to formulate strategies that capitalize on strengths, address weaknesses, seize opportunities, and mitigate threats.

3. Stakeholder Engagement and Collaboration

Successful strategic consulting extends beyond boardroom discussions; it involves engaging with key stakeholders across the organization. Consultants seek input from employees, management, and other stakeholders to gain diverse perspectives.

Collaboration fosters a sense of ownership and ensures that the strategic initiatives resonate with those responsible for their implementation.

4. Scenario Planning

The business environment is dynamic, and strategic consultants recognize the importance of scenario planning.

Consultants develop multiple scenarios to anticipate various future outcomes and devise strategies that are robust and adaptable. This approach helps organizations proactively respond to changing market conditions and unexpected challenges.

5. Agile Methodologies

Agile methodologies, derived from software development practices, have found their way into strategic consulting.

Embracing an iterative and adaptive approach, consultants implement Agile methodologies to enhance flexibility and responsiveness. This iterative cycle of planning, execution, and evaluation allows for quick adjustments based on real-time feedback.

6. Blue Ocean Strategy

The Blue Ocean Strategy, introduced by W. Chan Kim and Renée Mauborgne, encourages organizations to explore untapped market spaces rather than competing in existing markets.

Consultants employing this approach help clients identify new opportunities, innovate offerings, and create uncontested market space, fostering innovation and sustainable growth.

7. Business Model Innovation

Strategic consultants often focus on business model innovation, reimagining how an organization creates, delivers, and captures value.

This approach goes beyond product or service innovation, exploring new revenue streams, partnerships, and customer experiences.

Business model innovation is a transformative strategy that can lead to a competitive edge in the market.

8. Digital Transformation Strategies

In the age of digitalization, strategic consultants emphasize digital transformation as a crucial approach. This involves integrating technology to optimize processes, enhance customer experiences, and stay ahead of industry trends.

Digital transformation strategies enable organizations to remain agile and competitive in the digital landscape.

9. Change Management and Communication

Implementing strategic initiatives often involves significant organizational change. Consultants adopt change management principles to guide clients through transitions smoothly.

Clear communication, stakeholder involvement, and addressing resistance are integral components of a successful change management strategy.

10. Continuous Evaluation and Improvement

A strategic consulting approach doesn't conclude with the implementation of strategies; it extends to continuous evaluation and improvement.

Consultants work closely with clients to monitor the effectiveness of implemented strategies, gather feedback, and make necessary adjustments.

This iterative process ensures that strategies remain aligned with organizational goals and evolving market dynamics.

11. Risk Management Strategies

Every strategic plan carries inherent risks, and consultants integrate risk management strategies into their approaches.

This involves identifying potential risks, assessing their impact, and developing contingency plans. By proactively addressing risks, consultants help organizations navigate uncertainties and mitigate potential setbacks.

In conclusion, strategic consulting approaches are diverse and adaptable, reflecting the multifaceted nature of the business landscape. Effective consultants tailor their approaches to the unique needs and challenges of each client, employing a combination of research, analysis, stakeholder engagement, and innovative methodologies. By embracing these strategic consulting approaches, organizations can position themselves not just to survive but to thrive in an ever-changing and competitive business environment.

Tailoring Solutions: Personalizing Your Consulting Approach for Client Success

The one-size-fits-all strategy is no longer appropriate in the fast-paced world of consulting.

Successful consultants understand the need of tailoring their consulting tactics to each client's specific difficulties, goals, and context.

This personalized method not only builds deeper customer connections, but it also guarantees that solutions resonate and produce actual results.

Understanding The Client's Landscape

A thorough grasp of the client's environment serves as the foundation for a specialized consulting strategy.

This entails more than simply market expertise; it necessitates an examination of the client's corporate culture, history, and unique pain areas.

Consultants must spend time developing connections, actively listening to stakeholders, and immersing themselves in the complexities of the client's business environment.

Customized Research And Analysis.
Instead of relying on general industry benchmarks, bespoke consulting entails undertaking personalized research and analysis.

This might entail conducting market research, analyzing competitors, and thoroughly reviewing internal procedures.

The purpose is to collect data particular to the client's condition, laying the groundwork for accurate and successful strategic suggestions.

Co-creation With Stakeholders

Successful consultants work in collaboration with important stakeholders. This collaborative method entails collaborating closely with the client's team to develop solutions.

By integrating stakeholders in the consulting process, consultants obtain useful insights, align strategies with organizational goals, and ensure that offered solutions are both practical and practicable in the client's operational environment.

Methodologies That Are Flexible
Customized consulting necessitates flexibility in methodology. Consultants should be willing to modify their tactics to meet the specific demands of each client.

Depending on the client's organizational structure, industry, and goals, this might include incorporating features from several approaches such as Agile, Design

Thinking, or Lean. The capacity to tailor approaches displays a dedication to client-centricity.

Addressing Specific Pain Points.

A critical part of personalizing solutions is addressing the client's individual pain spots. Consultants must go beyond the surface and investigate the underlying causes of problems.

By thoroughly knowing the client's pain areas, consultants may build tailored tactics that deliver long-term solutions rather than simply treating symptoms.

Personalizing Communication.

A specialized consulting strategy relies on effective communication. This includes both the content of the message and how it is delivered.

Consultants must modify their communication style to appeal to diverse stakeholders inside the client's business. Communication that is clear, open, and individualized promotes trust and collaboration.

Aligning With Organizational Culture.
Every organization has its own culture, beliefs, and methods of doing things. A customized consulting strategy reflects and respects the client's company culture.

This includes learning about the client's decision-making processes, communication conventions, and preferred modalities of cooperation.

Consultants that can easily blend into the client's culture are better positioned to generate good results.

Metrics And Key Performance Indicators (KPIs).
Tailored solutions are based on demonstrable results. Consultants collaborate with clients to

create particular metrics and key performance indicators that are consistent with corporate objectives. By setting specific success criteria, consultants and clients may objectively analyze the impact of implemented initiatives and make data-driven modifications as needed.

Training and Skills Transfer
Rather than providing solutions that rely on the consultant, a personalized strategy emphasizes training and skill transfer.

Consultants should aggressively transmit information and skills to the client's team, allowing them to maintain and expand on the existing tactics.

This long-term view guarantees that the customer can tackle future issues on their own. Continuous evaluation and adaptation.
A specialized consulting strategy does not conclude with the supply of solutions. Consultants participate in continual examination and adaptation.

Regular check-ins, feedback sessions, and assessments of plan efficacy are essential. This iterative method guarantees that the consulting strategy adapts to the client's changing demands and the dynamic external environment.

To summarize, customizing solutions is more than simply a consulting method; it is a dedication to customer satisfaction. Successful consultants acknowledge each client's individuality and welcome the challenge of tailoring their tactics accordingly. Consultants may provide solutions that are not only successful but also long-lasting by knowing the client's landscape, engaging in co-creation, modifying approaches, and regularly reviewing outcomes. In the consulting business, customisation is the key to helping clients achieve transformational and long-term success.

Staying Ahead of Trends: Adapting Strategies to Evolving Business Environments in Consulting

In the fast-paced and ever-changing landscape of business, staying ahead of trends is not just a competitive advantage but a necessity for consultants aiming to deliver impactful and relevant solutions.

The ability to adapt strategies to evolving business environments is a hallmark of successful consulting practices.

Here, we explore key principles and approaches that consultants employ to stay ahead of trends and proactively shape the future for their clients.

★ **Continuous Learning and Professional Development**: Staying ahead of trends begins with a commitment to continuous learning. Successful consultants prioritize professional development by staying informed about emerging technologies, industry best practices, and market dynamics.

This might involve attending conferences, participating in webinars, and actively seeking out opportunities for skill enhancement.

A consultant's ability to offer cutting-edge solutions is directly linked to their commitment to ongoing education.

★ **Market Research and Environmental Scanning**
A foundational element of staying ahead of trends is conducting thorough market research and environmental scanning. Consultants must immerse themselves in the client's industry, understand market trends, and anticipate shifts in consumer behavior.

This proactive approach enables consultants to provide insights that go beyond immediate needs, positioning clients to navigate future challenges.

★ **Networking and Collaboration**
Building a robust network and fostering collaborations with industry leaders are essential strategies for staying ahead of trends.

By actively engaging with professionals, thought leaders, and organizations, consultants gain valuable insights into emerging trends and innovative practices.

Networking facilitates the exchange of ideas, fosters collaborative opportunities, and provides a real-time understanding of industry shifts.

★ **Agility and Adaptability**
The ability to pivot and adapt quickly is a hallmark of successful consultants. Agility

is crucial in a business environment where change is constant.

Consultants must be willing to reassess strategies, modify approaches, and embrace new methodologies as trends evolve.

An adaptable mindset ensures that consultants remain responsive to the dynamic needs of their clients and the broader business landscape.

★ **Technology Integration**
Technology is a powerful driver of change in today's business world. Successful consultants leverage technology not only to streamline their own operations but also to offer innovative solutions to clients.

Whether it's implementing advanced analytics, artificial intelligence, or automation, consultants who integrate cutting-edge technologies into their strategies position themselves and their clients for success in a rapidly evolving digital landscape.

★ Data-Driven Decision-Making

Staying ahead of trends involves harnessing the power of data. Consultants who prioritize data-driven decision-making can identify patterns, predict market trends, and make informed recommendations.

This approach not only enhances the accuracy of strategic decisions but also enables consultants to provide clients with actionable insights based on real-time data.

★ Scenario Planning

Given the inherent uncertainties in business, scenario planning is a strategic tool for consultants. By envisioning and preparing for multiple future scenarios, consultants can proactively develop strategies that are resilient to different outcomes.

This forward-thinking approach ensures that clients are well-prepared to navigate uncertainties and capitalize on emerging opportunities.

★ **Client-Centric Innovation**

Innovation is a key driver of staying ahead of trends, and successful consultants prioritize client-centric innovation.

By actively seeking feedback from clients, understanding their pain points, and collaborating on innovative solutions, consultants can tailor strategies that not only address current challenges but also anticipate future needs.

Client-centric innovation fosters long-term partnerships and positions consultants as trusted advisors.

★ **Cultural Awareness and Global Perspective**

In a globalized business environment, consultants must be culturally aware and possess a global perspective.

Staying ahead of trends involves understanding the impact of cultural shifts, global events, and geopolitical changes on businesses.

This awareness allows consultants to offer strategies that are not only relevant but also considerate of the broader socio-cultural and economic context in which their clients operate.

★ **Strategic Foresight**

Strategic foresight is about anticipating future trends and positioning clients to capitalize on them.

Successful consultants engage in horizon scanning, trend analysis, and foresight exercises to identify emerging opportunities and challenges.

By developing a strategic foresight mindset, consultants can guide clients toward sustainable success by aligning strategies with future market dynamics.

★ **Investment in Thought Leadership**
Consultants who stay ahead of trends often invest in thought leadership. By actively contributing to industry discussions, publishing insightful content, and sharing expertise through various channels, consultants position themselves as industry leaders.

Thought leadership not only enhances a consultant's reputation but also provides a platform to influence and shape industry trends.

In conclusion, staying ahead of trends is not just a strategy for consultants—it's a mindset. Successful consultants proactively seek out knowledge, embrace agility, leverage technology, and actively collaborate to navigate the complexities of an ever-evolving business environment. By integrating these principles into their consulting practices, consultants not only stay ahead of trends but also position themselves as trusted partners for clients looking to navigate the future with confidence and foresight.

Chapter 4

Client Relationship And Networking

Building and sustaining excellent client connections is fundamental to effective consulting. Consultants who want to succeed long-term must be able to create rapport, understand client needs, and foster long-term collaborations.

Furthermore, successful industry networking opens up new chances for clients and collaborations. Here, we look at the importance of client interactions and networking in the consulting industry.

Client Relationship Management.

1. Understanding Client Needs

Consultants begin by extensively studying the client's business, industry, and unique difficulties.

This includes actively listening, asking insightful questions, and completing extensive research to obtain a clear grasp of the client's situation.

2. Clear Communication

Effective communication is critical. Consultants must communicate difficult ideas in a straightforward and understandable manner.

Transparent communication fosters trust and ensures that customers are informed and confident during the consultation process.

3. Reactive And Proactive

Being responsive to client questions and proactive in resolving any difficulties indicates dedication.

Consultants that go above and beyond to anticipate client needs and deliver timely answers enhance the client experience.

4. Creating Realistic Expectations.

Clear expectations are necessary. Consultants must explain realistic objectives, timetables, and outcomes.

This kind of openness fosters confidence and aids in managing client expectations during the consulting engagement.

5. Regular Check-ins

Regular contact, such as check-ins and progress reports, helps to establish a healthy customer connection.

These contacts offer chances to resolve problems, solicit input, and ensure alignment with changing client goals.

Networking for Consulting
1. Creating a Professional Network

Networking is critical to consultancy success. Building a wide professional network enables consultants to access a plethora of expertise, remain current with industry trends, and generate chances for cooperation.

2. Attending Industry Events.

Consultants are actively involved in industry conferences, seminars, and networking activities.

These events give an opportunity to network with possible clients, coworkers, and industry influencers. Participating in such events helps consultants create relationships and stay up to date on industry changes.

3. Utilizing Online Platforms

Online platforms are important tools for networking in the digital era. Social media, professional networking websites, and industry forums make it easier to interact with people all around the world.

Consultants use these platforms to share their knowledge, participate in debates, and broaden their reach within the business.

4. Collaboration with Peers

Collaboration with other consultants and professionals in adjacent sectors increases networking opportunities.

Establishing relationships with colleagues may result in joint initiatives, shared ideas, and a larger customer base.

5. Adding Value to Connections

Effective networking is about both what one can obtain and what one can provide.

Consultants who actively add value to their network, whether via information sharing, introductions, or joint efforts, form stronger and more reciprocal professional ties.

6. Seeking Client Referrals

Clients who are satisfied are effective advocates. Consultants that provide excellent service are frequently referred by clients.

Word-of-mouth referrals from satisfied clients may greatly broaden a consultant's network and attract new business prospects.

7. Professional Associations and Affiliates

Joining professional groups and affiliations in the consulting sector gives you access to a network of like-minded people.

These groups provide chances for networking, information sharing, and staying current on industry best practices.

8. Strategic Alliance

Consultants build strategic connections with other businesses or experts whose skills complement their own.

This collaborative approach broadens the services that consultants may provide and allows them to reach a larger customer base.

In *essence, client relationship management and networking are inextricably linked in the consulting business. Consultants that focus on understanding and addressing client needs, communicate effectively, and establish strong industry networks are well positioned for long-term success. Fostering client connections and actively engaging in strategic networking provide a solid basis for a flourishing consulting firm.*

Building Strong Client Relationships: The Key to Consulting Success

The ability to build and sustain excellent client connections is more than a talent in the fast-paced world of consulting; it is a need for success.

Understanding requirements, cultivating trust, and creating a collaborative atmosphere are all part of the process of developing long-term partnerships.

Here, we look at the importance of developing great client connections and the main techniques that consultants use to lay the groundwork for long-term success.

Understanding the Client's Need
1. Active Listening

The first step in building excellent customer connections is active listening.

Consultants must listen carefully to their customers in order to have a thorough grasp of their issues, goals, and aspirations.

This sympathetic approach creates the framework for individualized solutions that are appropriate for the client's specific situation.

2. Thorough Research

Beyond client contacts, consultants conduct extensive research to get insight into the client's industry, competitors, and market trends. This complete understanding helps consultants to make educated suggestions and establishes them as valued advisors rather than just service suppliers.

Clear Communication
1. Clear Expectations

Clear and clear communication is critical. Setting realistic expectations for project schedules, deliverables, and probable obstacles builds confidence.

Clients like consultants that communicate honestly and provide a clear plan for their consulting engagement.

2. Timely Updates

Continuous communication is essential throughout the consultation process. Consultants offer regular reports on project progress, milestones reached, and any changes to the original plan.

This proactive communication ensures that clients are fully informed and engaged in the collaborative process.

Building Trust
1. Consistent Delivery of Value

Trust is created by consistently delivering value. Consultants that consistently meet or exceed client expectations earn a reputation for dependability and expertise.

Each successful assignment helps to strengthen the overall credibility of the consultant-client relationship.

2. Integrity and Transparency

Consultants must preserve the highest levels of ethics and transparency. Admitting problems, delivering honest evaluations, and providing straightforward solutions in times of uncertainty all contribute to the development of trust.

Clients like consultants that promote honesty and integrity.

A Client-Centric Approach
1. Customized Solutions.

A client-centric strategy entails adapting solutions to the individual demands of the customer.

Consultants eschew a one-size-fits-all approach, acknowledging that each client faces distinct obstacles and goals. Customized solutions exhibit dedication to the client's success.

2. Understanding Organizational Culture.

Consultants study the client's company culture, values, and decision-making processes.

This insight enables consultants to tailor their techniques to the client's culture, resulting in a collaborative and amicable working relationship.

Proactive Problem Solving
1. Anticipating Needs

Building successful customer relationships entails not just satisfying present demands, but also predicting future issues. Proactive consultants anticipate clients' requirements and provide answers before problems emerge.

This foresight establishes consultants as strategic partners interested in the client's long-term success.

2. Agile Adaptation

In a continuously changing corporate world, consultants must be adaptable to shifting conditions. Flexibility in adapting techniques to new difficulties or possibilities displays a dedication to proactive problem-solving.

Following-up on the project
1. Feedback sessions

After completing a project, consultants hold feedback meetings with customers. This two-way connection allows customers to express their thoughts on the consulting process, while consultants acquire vital insights for continual development.

It also demonstrates the consultant's commitment to continuing engagement.

2. After-Project Support

Providing post-project assistance and coaching strengthens client relationships. Consultants provide materials, answer questions, and help customers execute recommended techniques.

This dedication to post-project assistance improves the entire customer experience..

Long-Term Relationship Development
1. Client Education

Consultants help companies understand industry trends, best practices, and upcoming technology.

This educational component promotes a long-term engagement in which clients see consultants not just as service providers but also as significant sources of industry expertise.

2. Strategic Planning For Future Collaboration.

Successful consultants strategize about future client engagements.

This might include recognizing possibilities for new projects, aligning with the client's long-term goals, and ensuring that the consultant stays a trusted adviser as requirements change.

The importance of trust and collaboration
Cultivating good customer connections is much more than just providing services; it's also about creating a culture of trust and collaboration.

Trust is the foundation of lasting partnerships, and consultants who emphasize creating trust through knowledge, communication, and continuous value delivery position themselves for long-term success.

Finally, cultivating good client connections is more than simply a great practice in consulting; it is an essential component of attaining long-term success. Consultants that emphasize client requirements, speak openly, establish trust, and handle difficulties proactively contribute to a pleasant client experience. These approaches foster long-term connections that not only lead to recurring business but also position consultants as important partners in their clients' success journeys.

Effective networking strategies in the consulting sector

Effective networking is a strategic need in the consulting industry, where contacts and connections are critical.

Building a strong network not only opens up new prospects, but it also increases a consultant's sector expertise and impact. In this section, we'll look at crucial networking tactics for consultants.

1. **Establish clear networking goals**: Before engaging in networking activities, consultants should establish clear objectives.
Whether it's extending the customer base, pursuing partnerships, or staying up-to-date on industry trends, having clear goals directs networking activities and ensures they correspond with professional goals.

2. Utilize professional organizations and groups: Joining appropriate professional associations and groups in the consulting sector provides a structured networking environment.

These organizations frequently hold conferences, events, and forums where consultants may network with colleagues, share insights, and remain current on industry changes.

3. Attend Industry Conferences and Events: Active participation in business conferences and events is an effective networking tactic. These meetings bring together experts, thought leaders, and prospective clientele.

Participating in debates, workshops, and networking events provides a great opportunity to broaden one's professional network.

4. Utilize online platforms: Online networking tools have become crucial in the digital era. LinkedIn, in particular, is a valuable resource for consultants.

Building a strong LinkedIn profile, joining relevant groups, and actively participating in conversations all help to create an online presence that draws connections and promotes professional engagement.

5. Establish thought leadership: Becoming a thought leader in a given field broadens networking prospects.

Consultants that constantly provide useful ideas, produce publications, or speak at industry events establish themselves as experts in their fields.

This visibility not only generates contacts, but also builds trust and credibility.

6. Seek And Be A Mentor.Building mentor-mentee ties is an effective networking tactic. Seasoned consultants can provide direction to individuals new to the sector, building professional relationships.

Simultaneously, being receptive to mentoring creates opportunities for learning and networking.

7. Participate in collaborative Projects:
Collaborative initiatives provide a natural venue for networking.

Collaborating with other consultants, professionals, or businesses on collaborative efforts not only broadens the network but also provides access to new viewpoints, talents, and clients.

8. Develop relationships, not transactions:
Instead of focusing exclusively on transactions, effective networking involves developing connections.

Consultants should focus on knowing others, actively listening, and establishing true connections. A relationship-centric strategy fosters long-term, mutually beneficial ties.

9. Attend Networking Events. Attend networking events expressly designed to help professionals connect.

These might vary from industry-specific mixers to more informal get-togethers.
Actively participate in talks, exchange business cards, and follow up with new contacts to strengthen ties.

10. Make Warm Introductions: Warm introductions made through shared ties have more weight than cold outreach.
Consultants should use their existing connections to broaden their network.

Requesting introductions from mutual contacts builds credibility and allows for more seamless networking encounters.

11. **Give Before You Receive**: Reciprocation is essential for effective networking. Before expecting anything in return, consultants should look for methods to add value to their networks.

This might include giving industry ideas, establishing introductions, or providing support. Giving increases goodwill and develops professional ties.

12. Use Alumni Networks: Many consultants have excellent ties with their alma mater. Leveraging alumni networks gives a common experience that may be used to develop professional relationships. Alumni gatherings and internet platforms provide opportunities to network with other graduates.

13. **Participate actively in industry forums**: Participating in industry-specific forums and discussion groups encourages networking within a certain community.

Active engagement in online forums or in-person meet-ups enables consultants to interact with like-minded individuals, share information, and broaden their network.
14. **Follow-up effectively** Networking activities should not stop after the initial connection.

Consultants should communicate with new contacts in a timely and tailored manner.

Expressing gratitude, repeating similar interests, and proposing future collaboration opportunities reinforces the original bond.

15. **Participate in workshops and training sessions:** Participating in seminars and training sessions provides an opportunity to meet professionals who have similar interests and aspirations.

These settings foster networking in a more concentrated and participatory manner. Effective networking in consulting is more than merely exchanging business cards and building superficial relationships.

It is about developing genuine relationships that lead to professional progress and success. By using these tactics, consultants may build a strong network that not only opens doors to possibilities but also deepens their knowledge,

increases their influence, and develops a sense of
community within the dynamic consulting
sector.

Using Social Media to Increase Client Engagement in Consulting

In the fast-paced, digitally-driven consulting market, harnessing social media is more than a trend; it is a strategic imperative.

Social media platforms enable consultants to engage with customers, promote their knowledge, and establish a strong online presence.

Here, we look at how consultants may use social media to improve client engagement and elevate their consulting firm.

1. Developing a Professional Profile:

Creating a professional and attractive profile on networks such as LinkedIn is the first step toward harnessing social media for client interaction.

A well-written profile should demonstrate expertise, highlight previous accomplishments, and give a clear value proposition to potential clients.

2. Sharing Thought Leadership Content:

Social media is a content-sharing tool that enables consultants to establish thought leadership in their industries.

Regularly publishing informative articles, industry trends, and case studies establishes consultants as experts in their field, attracting the attention of customers looking for knowledge.

3. Participating in Industry Conversations:

Participating in industry-related debates and discussions on social media platforms is an effective technique.

Consultants may interact with peers, clients, and industry influencers by sharing ideas, asking questions, and participating in relevant discussions.

This engagement not only broadens the network, but also improves exposure.

4. Demonstrating Successful Projects:
Social media offers a visual platform for promoting successful consulting initiatives.

To demonstrate their influence, consultants might present case studies, project highlights, and client testimonials. Visual material offers a dynamic aspect that makes it more appealing to potential clients.

5. Creating Educational Content:
Consultants may use social media to educate their audiences by developing and sharing useful material.

This can contain infographics, whitepapers, seminars, or short video clips that provide advice and insights. Educational material not only promotes consultants as experts, but it also adds concrete value to customers.

6. Use Targeted Advertising:

Social media networks provide powerful advertising features that enable consultants to target certain demographics, sectors, or geographical locations.

Consultants may reach out to potential clients and increase the exposure of their services by effectively using targeted advertising.

7. Networking And Relationship-building:

Social media allows people to network on a worldwide scale.

Consultants can use platforms like LinkedIn to engage with professionals, potential clients, and industry colleagues.

Building and sustaining relationships on social media may lead to collaborations and commercial partnerships.

8. Using Social Listening:

Social listening is keeping track of online conversations related to a consultant's area of expertise and industry.

Consultants may gain useful insights that shape their strategy and improve client engagement by staying on top of hot issues, debates, and attitudes.

9. Participating in Live Sessions:

Live sessions on platforms like as LinkedIn Live and Instagram Live provide a real-time and engaging approach to communicate with clients. Consultants can hold Q&A sessions, panel discussions, or provide live updates to their clients, creating a feeling of immediacy and authenticity.

10. Highlighting Company Culture:

Clients frequently desire an insight into the business culture of the consultants they hire.

Social media is an excellent forum for highlighting the human aspect of a consulting firm.

Sharing behind-the-scenes information, team accomplishments, and milestones helps to humanize the business and enhance customer connections.

11. Use Hashtags Strategically:

Using appropriate hashtags in social media posts improves discoverability. Consultants might utilize industry-specific or trendy hashtags to boost their content's exposure and attract clients looking for expertise in certain areas.

12. Encouraging Client Testimonials:

Social proof is an effective technique for customer engagement. Consultants can encourage delighted customers to post testimonials on social media.

Positive testimonials increase credibility and trust, influencing future clients who discover the consultant's profile.

13. Monitoring Metrics and Analytics:

The analytics capabilities supplied by social media sites are critical for improving strategy. Consultants should track metrics like engagement rates, follower demographics, and post performance to evaluate the efficacy of their social media campaigns and make data-driven changes.

14. Maintaining Consistency and Authenticity:

A strong social media presence requires consistent and authentic content.

Posting on a frequent and honest basis helps to ensure brand consistency and confirms the consultant's dedication to client involvement.

Authenticity builds trust and resonates with clients looking for true interactions.

15. Adapting To Platform Changes:
Social media networks often change their algorithms and functionalities.

Consultants should keep current on these developments and adjust their methods accordingly. Staying updated helps consultants make the most of each platform's potential for client interaction.

To summarize, social media is a dynamic instrument that, when used properly, may dramatically improve client engagement for consultants. Consultants may generate a strong online presence that connects with clients, promotes connections, and positions them as industry experts by carefully leveraging various platforms, distributing relevant material, creating contacts, and staying up to date on industry trends.

Chapter 5

Navigating Challenges in Consulting: Strategies for Success

The consulting industry is dynamic and demanding, requiring professionals to navigate a myriad of challenges to achieve success.

From evolving client expectations to managing complex projects, consultants face a landscape that demands resilience, adaptability, and strategic thinking.

Here, we explore common challenges in consulting and strategies for effectively navigating them.

1. Client Expectations and Satisfaction

Challenge: Meeting and exceeding client expectations can be demanding. Misalignment in expectations or changes in client priorities during a project can pose significant challenges.

Strategy: Establish clear communication from the outset. Define project scope, deliverables, and timelines transparently.

Regularly check in with clients, seek feedback, and be agile in adapting strategies to align with evolving expectations.

2. Managing Time and Resources

Challenge: Consultants often work on multiple projects simultaneously, requiring effective time and resource management. Balancing client demands, project deadlines, and maintaining high-quality work can be challenging.

Strategy: Prioritize tasks based on urgency and importance. Utilize project management tools to track progress, allocate resources efficiently, and ensure deadlines are met. Regularly reassess project timelines to accommodate unexpected challenges.

3. Handling Resistance to Change

Challenge: Implementing changes within client organizations may face resistance from employees. Overcoming resistance and ensuring smooth transitions are critical challenges.

Strategy: Invest in change management strategies. Clearly communicate the benefits of proposed changes, involve key stakeholders in the decision-making process, and provide support for employees adapting to new processes. Address concerns empathetically to foster a positive transition.

4. Maintaining Client Relationships

Challenge: Building and maintaining strong client relationships is an ongoing challenge.

Client turnover, changing leadership, or shifts in organizational priorities can impact relationship continuity.

Strategy: Focus on building long-term relationships. Understand the client's business thoroughly, deliver consistent value, and engage in regular communication. Continuously demonstrate your commitment to the client's success to foster enduring partnerships.

5. Scope Creep:

Challenge: Expanding project scopes without corresponding adjustments in timelines and resources can lead to scope creep.

This can strain consultant-client relationships and impact project outcomes.

Strategy: Clearly define project scopes and deliverables from the beginning. Implement change control processes to manage any proposed scope changes.

Communicate proactively with clients about the potential impact of scope changes on timelines and budgets.

6. Balancing Work-Life Commitments

Challenge: The consulting profession is notorious for its demanding schedules, leading to challenges in maintaining a healthy work-life balance.

Strategy: Set realistic expectations for workloads, delegate responsibilities when possible, and prioritize self-care.

Establish boundaries for work hours and downtime to prevent burnout. Communicate openly with clients about reasonable timelines for deliverables.

7. Adapting to Technology Changes

Challenge: The rapid evolution of technology requires consultants to continuously update their skills and adapt to emerging tools and platforms.

Strategy: Invest in ongoing professional development. Stay informed about industry trends, attend relevant workshops, and engage in continuous learning. Collaborate with tech experts within the team to stay ahead of technological advancements.

8. **Managing Team Dynamics**:

Challenge: Leading and managing diverse teams with varying skill sets, personalities, and working styles can be challenging.

Strategy: Foster a positive team culture by promoting open communication, recognizing individual strengths, and addressing conflicts promptly.

Encourage collaboration and ensure that team members feel valued and heard.

9. **Financial Pressures:**

Challenge: Consultants may face pressure to manage project budgets effectively, especially when unexpected challenges arise.

Strategy: Implement rigorous financial planning. Regularly monitor project budgets and expenses. Be transparent with clients about potential budget adjustments, and work collaboratively to find solutions that align with project objectives.

10. Crisis Management:

Challenge: Unforeseen crises, whether internal or external, can disrupt project timelines and deliverables.

Strategy: Develop comprehensive crisis management plans that outline immediate responses and long-term strategies.

Keep clients informed about challenges, mitigation plans, and steps being taken to ensure project success despite unexpected hurdles.

In conclusion, successfully navigating challenges in consulting requires a combination of strategic planning, effective communication, and adaptability.

By proactively addressing client expectations, managing resources efficiently, building strong relationships, and staying current with industry trends, consultants can not only overcome challenges but also thrive in an ever-evolving professional landscape.

Overcoming Common Challenges: A Resilient Approach to Consulting

In the dynamic world of consulting, professionals often encounter a spectrum of challenges that require resilience, adaptability, and strategic problem-solving.

Recognizing these challenges and implementing a resilient approach is crucial for sustained success in the consulting industry.

Here, we explore common challenges faced by consultants and strategies for overcoming them with resilience.

1. Client Expectations and Communication:

Challenge: Aligning client expectations with project deliverables and maintaining clear communication throughout the engagement can be challenging.

Resilient Approach: Establish transparent communication channels from the project's inception. Regularly check in with clients to ensure alignment, provide progress updates, and address concerns promptly.

A resilient consultant actively manages expectations and adapts strategies to evolving client needs.

2. Adapting to Change

Challenge: The consulting landscape is inherently dynamic, requiring consultants to adapt to rapidly changing client needs, industry trends, and technological advancements.

Resilient Approach: Embrace a mindset of continuous learning. Stay informed about industry shifts, invest in professional development, and be agile in adapting to change.

Resilient consultants view change as an opportunity for growth rather than a hindrance.

3. **Managing Time and Workload:**

Challenge: Balancing multiple projects and deadlines while maintaining quality work can lead to challenges in time and workload management.

Resilient Approach: Prioritize tasks based on urgency and importance. Implement effective project management tools, delegate responsibilities when necessary, and set realistic expectations for workloads.

Resilient consultants proactively manage their time to ensure optimal project outcomes.

4. **Navigating Internal and External Collaborations:**

Challenge: Collaborating with diverse teams, both internal and external, brings challenges related to different working styles, communication preferences, and expectations.

Resilient Approach:Foster a collaborative culture by promoting open communication, understanding diverse perspectives, and addressing conflicts promptly.

Resilient consultants actively build strong collaborative relationships and adapt their communication styles to meet the needs of various team members.

5. Budgetary Constraints:
Challenge: Meeting project objectives within tight budgets requires careful financial planning and effective resource allocation.

Resilient Approach: Implement rigorous financial planning, regularly monitor project budgets, and be transparent with clients about potential budget adjustments. Resilient consultants seek creative solutions to deliver value while adhering to budgetary constraints.

6. Client Turnover:

Challenge: Client turnover or changes in leadership can disrupt ongoing projects and impact client relationships.

Resilient Approach: Develop long-term relationships that extend beyond individual contacts. Stay informed about organizational changes within client companies, adapt to new client expectations, and actively demonstrate the ongoing value of consulting services.

Resilient consultants anticipate and navigate client transitions with flexibility.

7. Technology Evolution:

Challenge: The rapid evolution of technology requires consultants to continuously update their skills and adapt to emerging tools and platforms.

Resilient Approach: Embrace a commitment to lifelong learning. Stay current with technological advancements, collaborate with tech experts, and actively seek opportunities to integrate new technologies into consulting solutions.

Resilient consultants view technological evolution as a chance to enhance service offerings and stay competitive.

8. Unforeseen Crisis:

Challenge: Unpredictable crises, whether internal or external, can present significant challenges to project timelines and deliverables.

Resilient Approach: Develop comprehensive crisis management plans that outline immediate responses and long-term strategies.

Maintain open communication with clients during crises, and proactively address challenges with adaptable solutions.

Resilient consultants navigate unexpected hurdles with a focus on ensuring project success despite disruptions.

In essence, a resilient approach to consulting involves proactive problem-solving, continuous learning, and the ability to adapt to diverse challenges.

By acknowledging these common challenges and embracing resilience, consultants position themselves not only to overcome obstacles but to thrive in a profession that demands flexibility, innovation, and unwavering determination.

Turning Setbacks into Opportunities: Strategies for Resolving Consulting Issues

In the complex landscape of consulting, setbacks are inevitable, but the ability to transform these challenges into opportunities is what sets successful consultants apart.

Whether it's a project deviation, client dissatisfaction, or unforeseen obstacles, adopting strategic approaches can turn setbacks into catalysts for growth.

Here, we explore effective strategies for resolving consulting issues and leveraging them as stepping stones toward success.

1. Root Cause Analysis

Strategy: When faced with setbacks, start by conducting a thorough root cause analysis. Identify the underlying factors contributing to the issue.

This analysis provides a clear understanding of the challenges at hand, allowing consultants to develop targeted solutions.

2. Proactive Communication:

Strategy: Transparent and proactive communication is key when addressing setbacks. Keep clients informed about the situation, provide insights into the challenges faced, and outline the steps being taken to resolve the issue.

Open communication fosters trust and demonstrates a commitment to addressing concerns collaboratively.

3. Agile Problem-Solving:

Strategy: Embrace an agile problem-solving mindset. Consultants should be prepared to adapt strategies quickly in response to unforeseen challenges.

Agility allows for rapid adjustments and ensures that setbacks do not impede the overall progress of a consulting engagement.

4. Client Collaboration:

Strategy: Turn setbacks into opportunities for strengthened client collaboration. Involve clients in the resolution process, seek their input on potential solutions, and showcase a commitment to working together to overcome challenges. Collaboration not only resolves issues but deepens the client-consultant partnership.

5. Continuous Learning:

Strategy: Treat setbacks as learning opportunities. Analyze the factors that led to the issue and incorporate lessons learned into future consulting practices.

Consultants who approach setbacks with a commitment to continuous learning are better positioned to prevent similar challenges in future engagements.

6. Adaptation to Change:
Strategy: Setbacks often signal the need for change. Embrace the opportunity to adapt and evolve consulting approaches.

Whether it's updating methodologies, incorporating new technologies, or refining project management strategies, consultants who adapt to change proactively position themselves for long-term success.

7. Client Feedback Integration:

Strategy: Turn setbacks into opportunities for soliciting and integrating client feedback.

Use setbacks as a catalyst for understanding client expectations more deeply. Encourage open dialogue about areas for improvement, and actively incorporate feedback into the consulting process for continuous enhancement.

8. Team Collaboration and Motivation:
Strategy: In the face of setbacks, foster a collaborative team environment. Encourage open communication within the team, share insights, and motivate team members to collectively address challenges.

Team collaboration not only resolves immediate issues but builds a resilient foundation for future projects.

9. Strategic Risk Management:
Strategy: Setbacks often arise from unforeseen risks. Develop and implement robust risk

management strategies that proactively identify potential challenges.

By addressing risks before they escalate, consultants can minimize the impact of setbacks and maintain project momentum.

10. Client Relationship Reinforcement:
   Strategy: Seize setbacks as opportunities to reinforce client relationships. Demonstrating resilience, commitment, and a solution-oriented approach during challenging times strengthens the client's confidence in the consultant's capabilities.

Clients who witness effective issue resolution are more likely to become long-term partners.
11. Innovation in Solutions:
   Strategy: Use setbacks as a catalyst for innovation. Explore creative solutions that go beyond conventional approaches.

Consultants who approach setbacks with a mindset of innovation can discover unique strategies that not only resolve immediate issues but also differentiate them in the market.

12. Post-Setback Evaluation:

Strategy: After resolving a setback, conduct a comprehensive evaluation. Analyze the effectiveness of the solutions implemented, identify areas for improvement, and document insights for future reference.

This post-setback evaluation contributes to ongoing professional growth and development.

13. Building Resilience:

Strategy: Develop a resilient mindset within the consulting team. Encourage team members to view setbacks as temporary challenges rather than insurmountable obstacles.

Building resilience at both an individual and team level contributes to a culture that thrives in the face of adversity.

14. Client Education on Solutions:

Strategy: Educate clients on the solutions implemented to address setbacks. Clearly communicate the steps taken, the impact on project outcomes, and the measures in place to prevent similar issues.

Client education builds transparency and reinforces the consultant's commitment to delivering quality results.

15. Celebrating Successes Amid Challenges:

Strategy: Acknowledge and celebrate successes, no matter how small, achieved in the aftermath of setbacks.

Recognizing and highlighting positive outcomes fosters a positive team culture and motivates consultants to approach challenges with resilience and determination.

In conclusion, turning setbacks into opportunities requires a strategic and proactive approach. By adopting these strategies, consultants can navigate challenges effectively, learn from setbacks, and ultimately strengthen their consulting practice. Resilience, adaptability, and a commitment to continuous improvement are the cornerstones of success in a dynamic consulting landscape.

Chapter 6

Scaling your consulting business: practical strategies for sustainable growth.

Scaling a consulting business entails more than simply extending client portfolios; it necessitates a deliberate approach that ensures long-term success, operational efficiency, and client pleasure.

As consultants transition from sole practitioners to strong businesses, here are practical and innovative ways for effectively increasing your consulting practice.

1. **Clarify your area and skill before scaling**. Determine the industries, services, or problem-solving areas where you shine.

A well-defined niche not only identifies your consulting firm, but also attracts clients looking for specific skills.

2. **Use Technology to Improve Efficiency**: Utilize technology to streamline operations and increase efficiency. Implement project management software, CRM systems, and communication platforms to improve collaboration and communication.

Technology not only enhances internal procedures, but it also helps to provide high-quality services to clients.

3. Create a Strong Online Presence: Build a strong online presence to reach a larger audience. Invest in a good website, optimize it for search engines, and generate compelling content that highlights your skills.

Use social media carefully to communicate with new clients, provide relevant insights, and increase brand recognition.

4. Create a Scalable Service Delivery Model: Create a service delivery model that can expand without sacrificing quality.

Standardize processes, provide reproducible frameworks, and define explicit workflows. This scalability ensures that your consulting business provides continuous service even as it grows.

5. Invest in Marketing and Branding: Allocate resources to these projects. Create an engaging brand message, invest in focused marketing initiatives, and actively participate in thought leadership activities.

A strong brand presence not only attracts new clients but also strengthens your consulting firm's trustworthiness.

6. **Identify and create strategic alliances that complement your services:** Collaborate with companies or experts whose expertise is relevant to your niche.

Strategic collaborations can help you broaden your service offerings, get access to new markets, and improve your entire value proposition.

7. **Build a High-Performing Team**: Scaling requires building a high-performing team. Hire people that have complimentary skills, shared beliefs, and are dedicated to your consulting firm's objective.

A cohesive team leads to better service performance and client satisfaction.

8. **Prioritize client management** through efficient communication and relationship development tactics: Check in with clients on a regular basis, get feedback, and show that you are proactive in dealing with their changing demands.

Strong client relationships foster recurring business and positive referrals.

9. **Diversify and Build Scalable Revenue Streams:** Investigate new service offerings, build online courses, or design products that complement your consulting experience.

Scalable revenue streams improve financial stability and resilience amid market swings.

10. **Embrace Data-Driven Decision Making**: Use data analytics to make strategic decisions. Analyze customer feedback, project performance, and market trends to discover growth possibilities and areas for improvement.

Data-driven decision-making guarantees that your consulting firm adjusts to shifting circumstances with precision.

11. **Prioritize Client Retention:** Building great relationships with current clients is just as important as obtaining new ones.

Use client retention methods include loyalty programs, regular communication, and value-added services. Clients that are satisfied become devoted advocates, which helps the firm thrive over time.

12. **Create an effective financial system** for managing revenue, expenses, and profitability.

Implement accounting software, monitor important financial KPIs, and create a solid budgeting plan. Clear financial systems promote budgetary responsibility and long-term growth.

13. **Customize consultation packages to meet client needs and budgets:** Offering a variety of

services enables you to appeal to a larger customer and tailor your offerings to different market segments.

14. **Continuously examine and optimize your pricing strategy:** Consider value-based pricing, tiered packages, or subscription models that are consistent with the perceived worth of your services.

A well-thought-out price structure guarantees that your consulting firm stays competitive and profitable.

15. **Prioritize professional development for yourself and your staff:** Keep up with current developments, attend relevant conferences, and engage in training programs.

Continuous learning guarantees that your consulting firm remains inventive and adaptive in a changing market.

16. **Implement Client Referral Programs**: Utilize delighted clients by offering referral programs. Offering incentives or special privileges to clients can encourage them to recommend your business.

Referral programs capitalize on favorable word-of-mouth, boosting your client base through trustworthy referrals.

17. **Explore strategic geographic growth depending on market need**: Determine which regions require your consulting services and tailor your company model to meet their needs.

This method enables you to enter new markets and broaden your consumer base.

18. **Monitor key performance indicators (KPIs)**:
Create and track key performance indicators for your consulting business.

Monitor measures such as client acquisition costs, customer lifetime value, and project success rates. Monitoring KPIs provides valuable insights into your company's overall health and performance.

19. **Create a Scalable Client Onboarding** approach:Establish an efficient approach for integrating new customers into your consulting ecosystem.

Standardized onboarding provides a consistent experience for clients while reducing the risk of oversight during the earliest stages of a client engagement.

20. **Regularly analyze and pivot your consulting firm** based on performance, market changes, and client feedback.

Be willing to adjust your strategies when circumstances change. Adaptability is a critical component of sustainable scaling, allowing your company to thrive in ever-changing conditions.

To summarize, scaling a consulting business necessitates a comprehensive and deliberate approach.

Consultants may confidently negotiate the hurdles of scaling by combining a well defined specialty, efficient operations, client-centric methods, and a dedication to continual development.

These practical techniques not only promote growth, but also help a thriving consulting firm achieve long-term success and resilience.

Strategies for Consultants to Maintain Work-Life Balance

Finding the right balance between work and life is a constant issue in the fast-paced, demanding consulting industry.

Short timelines, high customer expectations, and the need for ongoing learning are all common characteristics of consulting.

However, maintaining a healthy work-life balance is critical to long-term success and well-being. Here, we'll look at practical ways that consultants can use to strike a healthy balance between their professional and home lives.

Recognizing the Challenge: The first step in addressing work-life balance is to recognize its importance.

Consultants are generally enthusiastic about their profession, which might lead to overcommitment.

Understanding how a healthy lifestyle boosts productivity, creativity, and job satisfaction is critical.

1. Establish clear and realistic boundaries

Strategy: Establish clear boundaries between business and personal life. Set specific work hours and adhere to them as much as feasible.

Share these boundaries with clients, teammates, and yourself. Making a clear distinction between work and leisure time promotes burnout prevention and a healthier work-life balance.

2. **Prioritize self-care as a strategy**: Make self-care a priority in your daily routine. Regular exercise, enough sleep, and a healthy diet all improve physical and mental health.

Caring for yourself boosts your resilience, energy, and ability to overcome workplace problems.

3. **Time Management Strategy:** Use efficient time management approaches. Prioritize jobs based on their urgency and relevance, use productivity tools, and manage your time effectively.

Effective time management enables you to meet corporate duties without sacrificing personal time, giving you greater control over your calendar.

4. Understand the Art of Delegation Strategy:
Recognize that you do not have to do everything
yourself. Delegate duties according to each team
member's talents and abilities.

Effective delegation not only distributes effort
but also allows for growth within your team,
hence increasing total team efficiency.

5. Set Up A Support System Strategy: Build a
solid support network both inside and outside
the workplace. Maintain open contact with
coworkers, express your concerns, and seek
assistance as needed.

A supportive team and a network of friends and
family can provide emotional support and help
you overcome professional and personal
obstacles.

6. Learn To Say No When Required:
Overcommitting can lead to burnout and reduce
the quality of your work. Evaluate your
workload realistically and decline any

assignments that could jeopardize your capacity to maintain a healthy work-life balance.

7. Create Rituals for Transition Strategy: Create rituals that distinguish between work and personal life. Whether it's a routine for completing work at the end of the day or a morning ritual to get your day started, these habits help you establish psychological boundaries that allow you to balance your professional and personal duties.

8. Create reasonable client expectations
  Strategy: Communicate with your clients about realistic timescales and expectations. Communicate project milestones, anticipated challenges, and any constraints on your availability.

Managing customer expectations ahead of time promotes confidence while reducing the likelihood of last-minute requests that upset your work-life balance.

9. Implement a Remote Work Flexibility Strategy: When possible, take advantage of remote job opportunities. Many consulting duties can be completed remotely, giving you more flexibility in your work schedule.

Negotiate with customers to include remote work options that are consistent with project goals and promote a more balanced lifestyle.

10. Schedule downtime: Plan relaxation into your calendar. Downtime should be deemed non-negotiable, whether for brief breaks during the day or extended periods for vacations or personal interests.

Schedule downtime to ensure you have time to relax and rejuvenate.

11. Boundary-based Continuous Learning Strategy: Accept constant learning, but set limits. While staying current with industry advancements and developing your skill set is crucial, make specific time for learning rather than allowing it to absorb every part of your life. Strive for a mix of study and relaxation.

12. **Create A Tech Detox Strategy:** Recognize how technology impacts your work-life balance. Set aside time for a technical detox, in which you disconnect from professional emails and communications.

This method helps to free up mental space for personal life by removing frequent professional distractions.

13. **Define your long-term personal and professional goals.**

Strategy: Determine your long-term personal and professional goals. This includes establishing what work-life balance means to you in relation to your career path.

Aligning short-term efforts with long-term objectives gives a sense of purpose and direction.

14. **Establish a Positive Workplace**:
Strategy: Establish a favorable and appropriate environment for your consulting efforts. Make sure your desk is neat, comfy, and conducive to focus.

Having a designated workstation helps to differentiate between professional and personal environments.

15. **Evaluate and adjust consistently Strategy**: Evaluate your work-life balance on a regular basis and be open to explore new techniques as needed. Recognize that the balance is dynamic and may require adjustment in response to changing conditions. Adaptability is essential for finding balance in your consulting profession.

Conclusion: *Consultants seek for a work-life balance. Implementing these practical tactics will allow you to take a more long-term perspective to your career and personal duties.*

Navigating Tomorrow: Consulting's Future Trends

The consulting landscape is ever-changing, influenced by technological improvements, shifting client expectations, and global shifts.

As consultants adjust to a quickly changing environment, getting ahead of future trends is critical for long-term success.

Here, we look at important themes influencing the future of consulting and how professionals can position themselves to prosper in this transformational period.

1. **Digital Transformation and Technology Integration:** The consulting sector is greatly impacted by the continuing digital revolution. Consultants are becoming increasingly important in supporting firms through their digital transformation initiatives.

This entails integrating emerging technologies like artificial intelligence, machine learning, blockchain, and data analytics to improve efficiency, innovation, and overall corporate performance.

As the demand for digital expertise grows, consultants must constantly refresh their skill sets to stay on top of technology-driven consulting solutions.

2. **Remote and Hybrid Work Models**: Global events have accelerated the trend of remote work, changing the way consulting services are offered. Future trends show a sustained emphasis on flexible work arrangements, including hybrid

models that combine remote and on-site engagements.

To succeed in this changing work environment, consultants must adapt to new collaboration tools, virtual communication platforms, and effective project management tactics.

3. Changing Client Expectations: Customers' expectations are shifting beyond traditional consulting methods.

Clients are now looking for partners who not only give solutions but also offer strategic insights and new ideas. Future consultants must understand their clients' industries, anticipate issues, and provide proactive, specialized solutions.

Building long-term relationships and delivering value beyond transactional services will be critical.

4. Data Privacy and Ethical Consulting: With a growing reliance on data-driven insights, consultants must address data privacy and ethical concerns.

Future consulting trends will emphasize the value of ethical decision-making, appropriate data utilization, and adherence to changing legislation.

Consultants will need to incorporate ethical issues into their suggestions and help customers navigate the complex world of data stewardship.

5. Emphasis on Sustainability and Social Impact: Consulting priorities are shifting towards corporate social responsibility and sustainability. Clients are looking for help incorporating environmental, social, and governance (ESG) considerations into their business plans.

Future consultants must be knowledgeable about sustainable practices, climate risk assessments, and strategies that correspond with societal and environmental objectives.

6. Resilience and Crisis Management: Consultants with experience in these areas are crucial due to global uncertainties and catastrophes.

The ability to negotiate unexpected obstacles, create crisis response strategies, and guide organizations through difficult times will be critical.

Future consultants should develop abilities in risk management, scenario planning, and crisis communication in order to provide valuable help during times of disturbance.

7. Industry-specific Knowledge

As sectors become more specialized, consultants with extensive industry knowledge will be in great demand. Future trends point to a shift towards consultants who can provide specialized expertise in niche sectors, addressing distinct issues and possibilities within certain businesses.

Continuous learning and industry immersion will be critical for consultants wanting to build out a niche in specific fields.

8. **Agile Approaches And Flexibility**: Agile approaches, originating from software development processes, are gaining popularity in consulting.

Future consultants will need to embrace agile, iterative problem-solving, and adaptable project management techniques.
The ability to pivot rapidly, respond to changing client demands, and provide incremental value will set effective consultants apart in the coming years.

9. **Augmented and Virtual Reality Solutions:**The integration of augmented reality

(AR) and virtual reality (VR) technology is gaining importance in consulting engagements.

These technologies provide immersive experiences, allowing consultants to convey difficult data, simulate scenarios, and increase client understanding.

Future consultants will need to investigate how AR and VR may be used to generate compelling solutions and presentations.

10. **Consulting for Diversity, Equity, and Inclusion (DEI).**
The emphasis on diversity, equity, and inclusion is increasing, and customers are looking for advice on how to create more inclusive workplaces.

Future consultants should understand DEI principles, cultural sensitivity, and ways for promoting diversity inside organizations. Consultants who can assist companies in developing inclusive cultures will be critical to the future workforce dynamics.

11. **Commitment to Continuous Learning and Professional Development**: The fast-paced nature of consulting requires a commitment to ongoing learning. Future consultants must focus on professional growth, keeping up with evolving trends, technologies, and market upheavals. Continuous education, certifications, and industry networks will be critical to staying competitive in the changing consulting landscape.

12. **Cross-Disciplinary Collaboration**

Future consulting trends hint to more cross-disciplinary collaboration.

Consultants will need to collaborate effectively with professionals in a variety of sectors, including technology, marketing, finance, and sustainability.

Interdisciplinary collaboration broadens the range of options and helps experts to solve complicated situations more effectively.

Conclusion
Navigating the future of consulting necessitates a proactive mindset and a dedication to staying ahead of emerging trends.

Successful consultants will embrace digital change, adapt to changing client expectations, and develop competence in fields such as data privacy, sustainability, and crisis management. Consultants can position themselves for long-term success in an ever-changing business landscape by always learning, remaining nimble, and cultivating a thorough awareness of industry dynamics.

Upholding Consultancy Ethics: Building Trust and Integrity

In the world of consulting, ethics are critical in shaping the profession's credibility, retaining client confidence, and cultivating long-term partnerships.

Ethical considerations are integrated into the fabric of every consulting engagement, guiding consultants' decision-making processes and guaranteeing the highest level of professionalism.

Here, we look at the ethics of consultancy, analyzing the ideas that underpin the sector and how consultants might negotiate ethical problems with integrity.

1. Client Confidentiality Principle: Maintaining client anonymity is a cornerstone of ethical consulting. Consultants are entrusted with sensitive information regarding their clients' operations, strategies, and issues.

Respecting and safeguarding this information is critical for establishing and maintaining confidence.

Consultants must develop explicit standards for managing confidential data, both digital and physical.

This includes safeguarding data, restricting access to authorized workers, and gaining explicit client authorization before sharing any non-public information.

2. Objective and impartial advice:

Principle: Providing objective and impartial counsel is an ethical requirement for consultants.

Objectivity guarantees that suggestions are based on unbiased analysis rather than personal interests, allowing clients to make more informed choices.

Guidelines: Consultants should avoid conflicts of interest and disclose any potential biases.

The pursuit of impartiality in assessments, recommendations, and decision-making processes displays a dedication to the client's best interests.

3. **Principle**: Ethical consultants promote competence and ongoing professional development.

Maintaining a high degree of competence in their sector allows consultants to provide customers with valuable, up-to-date insights.

Advice: Consultants should invest in continuing education, training, and skill development. Keeping up with industry trends, developing technology, and best practices enables consultants to provide relevant and effective solutions.

4. **Principle**: Transparency and Honest Communication. Ethical consultants value open and honest communication.

Openly sharing information, including potential obstacles and constraints, promotes confidence between consultants and clients.

Consultants should communicate simply, eliminate jargon, and ensure that clients understand the ramifications of their advice.

Being open about potential risks, uncertainties, and the viability of proposed solutions promotes a transparent and ethical consultation process.

5. Client Welfare and Benefits:
  Principle: In ethical consulting, the client's well-being and benefit should come first.

Consultants are engaged to provide value for clients, and ethical behavior entails putting the client's interests ahead of the consultant's.
  Guidance: Consultants should consider how their advice may affect the client's overall welfare.

Prioritizing long-term advantages and sustainability over short-term gains is consistent with ethical standards and leads to better client outcomes.

6. **Principle**: Integrity in business relationships. Ethical consultants must establish and maintain honesty in all business dealings. This includes

encounters with customers, coworkers, vendors, and other stakeholders.

Consultants should maintain the greatest levels of honesty, impartiality, and integrity in their relationships. Maintaining a reputation for ethical behavior boosts credibility and helps to build long-term professional partnerships.

7. Social Responsibility and Sustainability: Ethical consultants understand their role in achieving societal goals.

This includes taking into account the social and environmental implications of their recommendations, as well as supporting sustainable practices.

Guidance: Consultants should incorporate social responsibility and sustainability into their suggestions.

This could include evaluating the environmental impact of suggested policies, encouraging diversity and inclusion, and supporting community efforts.

8. **Principle**: Ethical consultants avoid unfair competition activities. This includes avoiding activities that could hurt competitors, leveraging confidential information, or using unethical marketing methods.

Guidance: Consultants should compete fairly and ethically, respecting the intellectual property and confidentiality of others.

Maintaining ethical competition procedures promotes a thriving and respected consulting sector.

9. Responsiveness to Changing Circumstances:
Principle: Ethical consultants can change and respond to changing situations.

This entails reassessing advice in response to changing customer needs, industry trends, or unexpected challenges.

Consultants should be flexible and willing to adapt their approaches in response to changing conditions.

A commitment to responsiveness displays a desire to provide the best results for clients in dynamic situations.

10. Ethical consultants carefully manage conflicts of interest: This includes recognizing and addressing situations in which personal or professional interests may jeopardize objectivity.

Guidance: Consultants should have processes in place to detect and resolve possible conflicts of interest.

This may involve disclosing relationships that may impair objectivity and collaborating with clients to resolve any perceived conflicts.

Maintaining consulting ethics is a professional duty that fosters long-term partnerships and contributes to the industry's integrity.

Consultants that prioritize client confidentiality, offer impartial advice, invest in ongoing professional development, communicate openly, and value social responsibility help to foster an ethical culture.

Adhering to these principles not only allows consultants to negotiate ethical problems with honesty, but it also ensures the profession's sustainability and reliability.

Critical And Effective Questions To Consider Asking During Consultation

Certainly! Here's a comprehensive list of critical and effective questions to consider asking during a consultation, covering many aspects of the client's business and goals.

Understanding Client Needs

1. What specific difficulties or pain areas are you now having in your business?

2. How would you describe your organization's current condition and operations?

3. Could you please define your immediate and long-term goals for this project or engagement?

4. What motivated you to seek consulting services at this time?

5. How do you see our collaboration's success?

Assessing Industry and Competition

6. How would you define the competitive environment in your industry?

7. What distinguishes your organization from competitors, and what challenges do you face?

8. Are you aware of any impending trends or disruptions in your industry that are particularly relevant?

9. How do you stay current with industry advancements, and what impact do they have on your strategy?

10. Could you possibly provide insight into your current market positioning and client perceptions?

Strategic Objectives

11. What are your primary business objectives for the next 1-3 years?

12. How do you prioritize your strategic goals, and what criteria do you apply?

13. Can you share any previous successes or challenges in synchronizing strategy and execution?

14. What indicators or metrics do you use to monitor progress toward your strategic goals?

15. How do your present strategies link to your organization's bigger goal and vision?

Operating Excellence

16. What are your organization's key operational processes?

17. How do you ensure consistency and quality in your operational workflows?

18. Do you believe any specific areas of your business could be more efficient?

19. What technology or tools are employed in your daily operational processes?

20. Could you give examples of beneficial process modifications you've done in the past?

Financial Landscape:

21. How do you currently manage budgeting and financial resources in your organization?

22. What are your key revenue streams, and how do you allocate resources across them?

23. Could you kindly elaborate on any financial concerns or limits that are currently influencing your decisions?

24. How do you approach financial forecasting and risk management?

25. Which important financial performance indicators do you pay close attention to?

Change Management

26. How has your company historically dealt with change, and what have you learned?

27. What challenges or successes have you experienced in previous transformation initiatives?

28. How do you communicate and manage change at different levels within your organization?

29. Are there any cultural elements that could influence the implementation of new approaches or changes?

30. How do you evaluate the effectiveness of change initiatives inside your organization?

Client-Centered Focus

31. Do you understand your customers' or clients' needs and preferences?

32. What feedback measures are currently in place for gathering client insights?

33. How do you adjust your services to different customer segments?

34. How would you describe your average client experience, from awareness to post-purchase?

35. What strategies are in place to increase customer satisfaction and loyalty?

Technology and Innovation

36. How crucial is technology in your current operations, and how open are you to adopting new technologies?

37. Are any specific innovation or R&D activities currently underway?

38. How do you ensure the security and privacy of your digital assets and client information?

39. Could you provide examples of successful and challenging technological implementations?

40. What problems have you faced when implementing new technology or innovations?

Risk Management

41. How do you now recognize and analyze hazards inside your organization?

42. Can you provide instances of risk mitigation methods that are currently in place?

43. What contingency plans are in place for unanticipated disruptions or crises?

44. How does your organization balance risk-taking and risk-aversion?

45. Are there any industry-specific threats that you are especially concerned about right now?

Employee Engagement and Development

46. How do you measure employee happiness and engagement in your organization?

47. What initiatives or programs are in place to assist staff learn and grow?

48. How do you foster a healthy working culture while keeping morale high?

49. Could you please discuss your successful strategies for staff retention and talent management?

50. How do you handle employee fatigue and turnover?

Marketing And Branding

51. How is your brand now positioned in the market, and what is your unique value proposition?

52. Which marketing channels have been most successful for your company?

53. How do you evaluate the efficacy of your marketing efforts and track their progress?

54. How consistent is your brand's messaging across channels and touchpoints?

55. What techniques do you use to stay relevant and unique in your industry?

Legal and Compliance:

56. What legal and regulatory frameworks do you now operate under?

57. How do you ensure compliance with industry-specific regulations, and are there any challenges?

58. Are there any pending legal challenges or compliance issues that we should be aware of?

59. How do ethical considerations influence your decision-making process?

60. What steps are taken to keep staff informed about regulatory or compliance changes?

Collaborative Partnerships

61. Do you have any existing collaborations or partnerships in your portfolio, and how do they affect your overall success?

62. How do you handle collaboration with external stakeholders, and what criteria do you use when making decisions?

63. Could you give any examples of successful joint ventures or alliances?

64. How do you assess the worth and efficacy of your collaborations?

65. What criteria do you use to discover potential collaborators and partners?

Assessing success

66. How do you now evaluate the performance of your operations and projects?

67. Which key performance indicators (KPIs) are critical for your organization?

68. How often do you monitor and analyze performance indicators, and who is involved in this process?

69. Could you please share some concrete success stories or case studies with us?

70. How do you use client, employee, and stakeholder feedback to improve your performance?

Conclusion

In conclusion, the work of a wealthy consultant is varied and dynamic, requiring a distinct combination of experience, strategic thinking, and adaptability.

As we've looked into several aspects of this profession, it's clear that success in consultancy goes beyond financial benefits; it also requires a commitment to constant learning, customer happiness, and ethical procedures.

One major message is the value of expertise and specialization. Wealthy consultants frequently excel in specialized areas or niches, using their extensive knowledge to deliver important insights to customers.

This skill not only provides a competitive advantage, but it also demonstrates the consultant's commitment to mastering their craft.

As the corporate landscape changes, the ability to keep ahead of market trends and emerging technology becomes an important factor of success.

Strategic thinking is another distinguishing feature of a successful affluent consultant.

Navigating complicated business challenges takes more than just technical knowledge; it also necessitates the capacity to develop inventive methods.

A consultant's ability to analyze circumstances, find possibilities, and develop effective solutions distinguishes them.

Furthermore, the finest consultants recognize that success is more than just managing current difficulties; it is also about anticipating future challenges and proactively helping their customers toward long-term progress.

Adaptability arises as a frequent theme in the field of rich consulting. The corporate world is inherently dynamic, thus consultants must be adaptable to changes.

This adaptability goes beyond technical abilities and includes good communication, interpersonal skills, and the ability to create long-term client relationships. The capacity to modify solutions to different company cultures and systems demonstrates a consultant's adaptability and resilience.

Client pleasure is the ultimate measure of success in consulting. A wealthy consultant's reputation is based on the tangible impact they have on their customers' company.

Whether it's streamlining operations, optimizing procedures, or providing creative solutions, the consultant's ability to deliver quantitative value is critical to their long-term success.

Furthermore, developing great client connections builds trust and frequently leads to repeat business and recommendations, which are essential for long-term success in this profession.

Ethical considerations are critical in the conclusion of the affluent consultant's story. Consultants, as stewards of valuable knowledge and advisors to enterprises, must maintain the highest ethical standards.

Confidentiality, avoiding conflicts of interest, and offering honest, clear counsel are all non-negotiable values.

Take note, a wealthy consultant's success is judged not only by financial gain, but also by the beneficial impact they make on their clients and the larger business community.

Finally, the path of a wealthy consultant is distinguished by a dedication to competence, strategic thinking, adaptability, customer satisfaction, and ethical behavior. Beyond the financial rewards, the true measure of success is a consultant's lasting impact on the company they assist. As industries evolve and new difficulties emerge, the job of the rich consultant will become increasingly important in creating business futures and contributing to the global economy's overall growth and prosperity.